5 WHYS:

THE EFFECTIVE ROOT CAUSE ANALYSIS

Oliver Roderich

ISBN: 9798708512604

“Improve quality, you automatically improve
productivity.”

W. Edwards Deming

TABLE OF CONTENTS

WELCOME

Hello, how are you? I would like to thank you, reader, for devoting part of your time to reading this book. Enjoy it!

Oliveir Roderich

1 INTRODUCTION

Usually when we identify a problem, the first thing we try to do is to carry out an action plan to correct it, spending time and resources on that solution. Often the proposed solution does not solve the problem because it does not eliminate the root cause. With that we only minimize the problem, where it may occur again in the future.

And do you also put out fires in the workplace? Have you ever been in a situation where you just minimized the problem and it happened again?

If so, you probably didn't eliminate the main reason that was causing the problem and spent time and resources on that initial solution.

Often, we can only see the symptoms, but not the root cause, the one that, if solved, the problem will be corrected once and for all.

In the work environment we need to ask ourselves to know more about what is actually happening in the process. Have you ever wondered why a problem happened?

HOW THE BOOK IS ORGANIZED

The book is divided into 3 topics, where **topic 1** presents a vision of what the 5 whys are, some application examples and when to use it in your day to day.

Topic 2 presents the step by step for you to elaborate and apply the 5 whys, from meeting with the team understanding what problems will be analyzed, to generating the necessary actions to eliminate the root cause of a problem.

Topic 3 presents an example, where you will have the opportunity to see the application of the knowledge learned in the previous topics and be encouraged to apply the 5 whys to a real problem in your work environment or in personal life.

Good reading!

2 WHAT IS THE 5 WHY TECHNIQUE?

The technique was initially developed at Toyota in order to improve processes and solve problems. It is widely used both in industry and in the service area, in addition to being a tool closely linked to continuous process improvement and lean methodology.

But before explaining this technique you must understand the concepts of problem and root cause:

Problem: It is a gap between what is expected and the current situation of a process.

- **Expected:** to produce 50 pieces / hour.
- **Current situation:** produces only 35 parts / hour.
- **Gap:** 15 pieces per hour.

Root cause: It is the main cause that caused a non-conformity (problem).

Briefly, the 5 why is done as follows: After defining the **problem or a non-conformity**, the team must ask itself why the situation occurred and then ask itself again in relation the answer given and so on until you reach the 5th why in order to find the **root cause** of the problem and thus eliminate it.

If we ask the question why repeatedly, we will be seeking to understand the problem clearly in order to actually find the main problem.

There is not always the need to ask yourself 5 times why. You should ask until **you identify the root cause of the problem** which can be 3, 4, 5, 6 times.

Some advantages of using the 5 whys to analyze a problem:

- Easy to use and can be applied on the shop floor;
- Low cost;
- Assists in identifying the root cause;
- Seeks everyone's participation in order to achieve a goal.

WHEN TO USE?

The 5 whys technique can be used in the following scenarios:

- Find the root cause of a problem;
- Understand why things happen within a process.
- Application in several areas such as: maintenance, quality, production, administrative areas, personal problems, among others.

We have already learned what 5 whys are,

their advantages and when to use them. But how do we perform the analysis of the 5 poquês? **Follow the step by step on the next pages and find out how to use this technique to generate ideas and solve problems.**

3 **5 WHYS**

To use the 5 whys technique you must follow the flow below, from meeting with the team to implementing the action plan to eliminate the root cause of the problem:

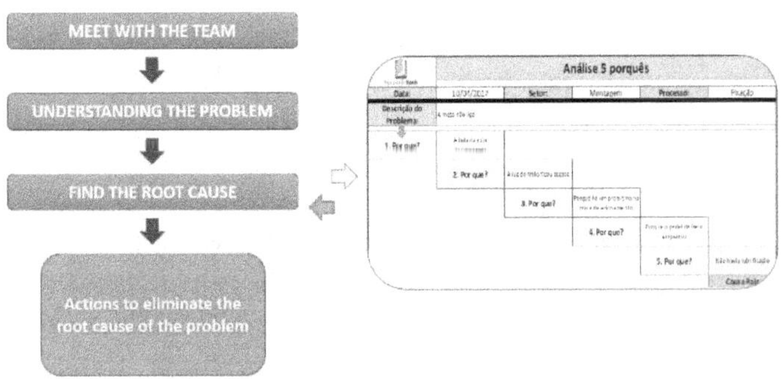

In the topics below, each step will be presented in more detail.

MEET WITH THE TEAM

Before starting to solve the problem, we must identify which sectors then involved in the process that presented a certain error.

Subsequently, we invite those responsible for the process and the people who carry out the activity that presented the problem.

It is very important that the entire team involved in the process is brought together. Think that the person responsible for each activity may have a different view, so that your experiences and points of view will help to achieve the results.

UNDERSTANDING THE PROBLEM

With the team together, it is time to set out to define the problem that needs to be solved, by understanding the following questions:

- How does the problem occur?
- What is the frequency of the error?
- Who carries out the activity?
- How is the activity carried out?
- Is there a working pattern for carrying out the activity?
- What factors can influence the error to happen?
- Are any processes being done improperly?

FIND THE ROOT CAUSE

With the help of the information gathered in the previous process, we move on to the next step, which is the identification of the root cause using the 5 whys technique.

Look for the answer for each reason based on facts that actually happened and not events that could have happened, in order not to be a deductive analysis according to the example below.

Resume Book	5 whys analysis		
Date:		Sector:	Process:
Description of the Problem:			
1. Why?			
	2. Why?		
		2. Why?	
			2. Why?
			2. Why?
			Root cause
Conclusion			

ACTION PLAN

Once the root cause is identified, the next step will be to structure an action plan to eliminate the root cause once and for all and prevent the problem from happening again.

To create the action plan you can use the

5w2h technique (what, who, why, when, where, how much and how), and then follow the progress of the action plan with your team measuring results and assessing whether the objective has been achieved.

FAILURE TREE

We can have more than one cause and sub-cause for a given process. For this we set up a fault tree applying the 5 whys in order to identify all possible causes of failure in a process, so when a problem occurs it is easy to identify where we should act to correct it.

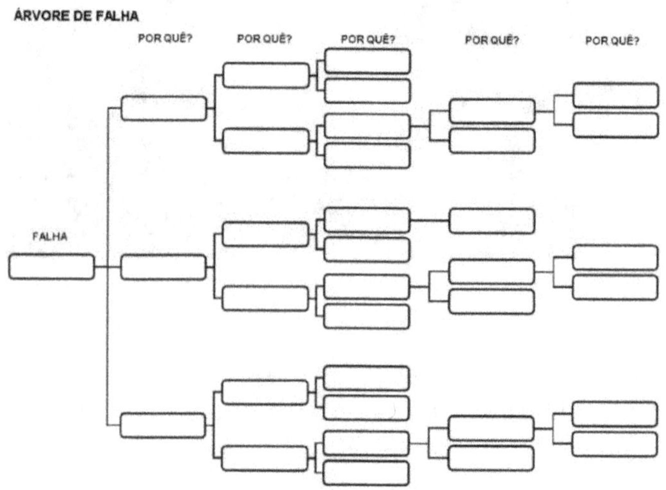

You noticed how simple the application of the 5 whys technique is. **Follow on the next pages a practical example of how to apply using a support worksheet to solve a problem.**

4 APPLICATION EXAMPLE

Below is an example of the application of 5 whys that tells the story of Carlos, a motorcyclist who uses his motorcycle to go to his work every day.

One day, Carlos started his motorcycle and realized that he didn't turn on any lights on the dashboard and his motorcycle wouldn't start.

Worried about the situation, Carlos took the motorcycle to the mechanic to evaluate what had happened where he used the 5 whys technique to solve this problem.

Initially, the mechanic understood the problem with Carlos, noted on the 5 whys analysis sheet and asked the first question to find out the first cause:

"Why doesn't the bike start?"

A: The battery is exhausted..

	5 whys analysis				
Date:	04/07/2020	Sector:	motorcycle	Process:	Ignition
Description of the Problem:	the motorcycle won't start				
1. Why?	The battery is discharged				

Evaluating the answer above, we could simply recharge the battery, or replace it to correct the problem, correct? .... Wrong! Observe the further analysis of the 5 whys and understand the importance of understanding the problem in depth.

After identifying the first cause, the mechanic charged the battery to perform more tests and did the analysis of the 5 whys once again:

"Why is the battery discharged?"

A: The brake light is on all the time consuming the battery.

	5 whys analysis				
Date:	04/07/2020	Sector:	motorcycle	Process:	Ignition
Description of the Problem:	the motorcycle won't start				
1. Why?	The battery is discharged				
	2. Why?	The brake light was on			

Evaluating the answer above, we verified that the problem was not with the battery, but with the brake light that was getting on, consuming the entire battery. Even if the mechanic changed the battery or charged it, it would be discharged after a few days because the mechanic would not eliminate the root cause of the problem.

With the previous analysis, the mechanic concluded that the problem was not in the battery, but in some component of the brake lighting system, so he performed the analysis of the 5 whys again, thus identifying the root cause of the problem.

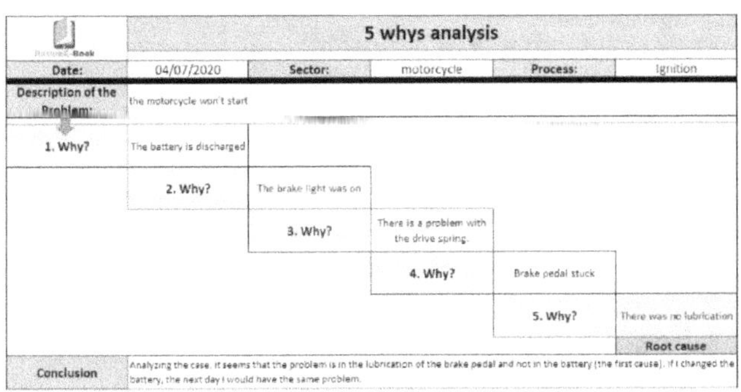

	5 whys analysis				
Date:	04/07/2020	Sector:	motorcycle	Process:	Ignition
Description of the Problem:	the motorcycle won't start				
1. Why?	The battery is discharged				
	2. Why?	The brake light was on			
		3. Why?	There is a problem with the drive spring.		
			4. Why?	Brake pedal stuck	
				5. Why?	There was no lubrication
					Root cause
Conclusion	Analyzing the case, it seems that the problem is in the lubrication of the brake pedal and not in the battery (the first cause). If I changed the battery, the next day I would have the same problem.				

After finishing the analysis, the mechanic concluded that the root cause was the **lubrication of the brake pedal**, which caused the pedal to become stuck, reducing the spring pressure in order to activate the warning light. brake, causing the battery to run out in such a way that it was not possible to start the motorcycle.

Therefore, it is important to understand the problem in depth and find the root cause to seek a definitive solution and avoid rework in the process.

There, the mechanic discovered the root cause. And now? We need to define measures to eliminate the problem once and for all so that it does not happen again. For this, the mechanic put together an action plan to correct Carlos' problem as shown below taking into account the root cause:

	5 whys analysis				
Date:	04/07/2020	**Sector:**	motorcycle	**Process:**	Ignition
Description of the Problem:	the motorcycle won't start				
1. Why?	The battery is discharged				
	2. Why?	The brake light was on			
		3. Why?	There is a problem with the drive spring.		
			4. Why?	Brake pedal stuck	
				5. Why?	There was no lubrication
					Root cause
Conclusion	Analyzing the case, it seems that the problem is in the lubrication of the brake pedal and not in the battery (the first cause). If I changed the battery, the next day I would have the same problem.				

Action Plan

What	How	Who	When	Where	Status
Lubricate the brake pedal	Disassemble the pedal and lubricate it with grease.	Patrick	15/abr	motorcycle mechanic	Plan
Charging the battery	using the battery charger	Patrick	15/abr	motorcycle mechanic	Plan
take the final test	Evaluate your pedal correctly apply the brake	Patrick	15/abr	motorcycle mechanic	Plan

When we find the root cause and actually eliminate the problem, we improve the company's result in relation to the team's productivity in order to avoid production stops to solve recurring problems in the process.

This time saved can be used to train the team, increase production or generate ideas for improvements in the process in order to eliminate other errors in the process.

APPLICATION

Did you like the 5 whys technique? Now it's your turn to apply the knowledge in your day to day. **Perform an analysis using the 5 whys technique with your team to solve a** problem in the root cause. It can be a problem for your company or your day to day. Remember to train your team on the 5 whys concepts to facilitate their realization.

	5 whys analysis				
Date:	04/07/2020	**Sector:**	motorcycle	**Process:**	ignition
Description of the Problem:	the motorcycle won't start				
1. Why?	The battery is discharged				
	2. Why?	The brake light was on			
		3. Why?	There is a problem with the drive spring.		
			4. Why?	Brake pedal stuck	
				5. Why?	There was no lubrication
					Root cause
Conclusion	Analyzing the case, it seems that the problem is in the lubrication of the brake pedal and not in the battery (the first cause). If I changed the battery, the next day I would have the same problem.				

Action Plan

What	How	Who	When	Where	Status
Lubricate the brake pedal	Disassemble the pedal and lubricate it with grease.	Patrick	15/abr	motorcycle mechanic	Plan
Charging the battery	using the battery charger	Patrick	15/abr	motorcycle mechanic	Plan
take the final test	Evaluate your pedal correctly apply the brake	Patrick	15/abr	motorcycle mechanic	Plan

Use the model of the 5 whys above to carry out the activity as presented previously in Carlos' case study.

5 **CONCLUSION**

Did you notice how simple and, best of all, effective the method is? The 5 whys, when done correctly, bring several benefits when you need to find the root cause of a problem and can be used by everyone in the company.

The more you apply the **5 whys** technique to solve day-to-day problems, the less problems will re-appear within your process in the short, medium and long term.

Start today using the 5 whys in your projects and processes you are working on. You will find that this tool will be very useful in your life, helping you to find the root cause of a problem and to seek solutions to the various problems that appear in your day.

Thank You!